Books by Sanora Babb

The Dark Earth and Selected Prose from the Great Depression
On the Dirty Plate Trail: Remembering the Dust Bowl Refugee Camps
Whose Names Are Unknown
Told in the Seed
Cry of the Tinamou: Stories
An Owl on Every Post
The Lost Traveler
The Dark Earth

About Sanora Babb

Unknown No More: Recovering Sanora Babb

Told *in the* Seed

and Selected Poems

Told *in the* Seed

and Selected Poems

SANORA BABB

MUSE INK PRESS

Muse Ink Press
1465 E. Putnam Avenue, Suite 529
Old Greenwich, CT 06870
www.sanorababb.com

Printed in the United States of America
ISBN 978-0-9859915-4-8
Designed by Ryan Ratliff

For Joanne

Contents

Introduction

Of all Sanora Babb's writings, it is the poetry, perhaps, that offers the most intimate and unvarnished picture of the woman and the artist. Although attention has largely focused on Babb as a writer of prose, she was an accomplished and successful poet first. She learned her craft during an era when American poetry was accessible and direct, when ordinary readers expected rhymed, metrical short verse to appear routinely in their morning papers and in general-interest magazines. At the same time, a boom in little literary magazines, both regional and national, provided a steady market for new verse. Over the years, Babb honed and polished her craft, turning from her early, rhymed poems of romanticized love and youthful exuberance toward a more modern, naturalistic style of poem and more serious subject matter. Throughout, she speaks directly to the reader, drawing imagery and subject matter from a lifetime of close observation and a strong affinity to the natural world. With an intimate and confiding voice, witty and alert to the pleasures of language and imagery even in grief, Sanora Babb's poems still stir the reader.

This new colleciton, *Told in the Seed and Selected Poems*, expands the original collection (sections I-IX) with selected poems (sections X-XIV) that cover her full range of poetry over the seventy years of her writing career. Despite her early and continued success as a poet, the body of work she produced has remained mostly out of sight. Many of the little magazines publishing Babb's poetry are defunct and have not been digitized. Others, like *Prairie Schooner* or *Arizona Quarterly*, are indexed and searchable online, assuming a reader knows to look there. Until now, though, readers wishing to know more of Babb's poetry beyond the thirty-six poems of the original *Told in the Seed* would have had to travel to the Harry Ransom Center in Austin, Texas, to search her papers. The thirty-nine poems newly collected here offer a sampling of her best work from every decade, with an emphasis on the late 1920s and 1930s, when Babb published dozens of accomplished lyric poems each year in regional and national magazines. Additional poems from the 1950s-1990s help flesh out our understanding of Babb's consuming interests as a poet, as well as her growth as a modern American poet. *Told in the Seed and Selected Poems* offers a representative record of her poetic oeuvre—and a key to understanding the poet herself.

The earliest poems also stand as a kind of record of an era of exciting new physical and professional freedom and opportunity for American women, particularly women in the western states, between the wars. After a year or two of college in Kansas, Babb found work in 1927 writing a column for the *Garden City Herald* and as an Associated Press stringer. She also made good use of the contemporary appetite for poetry, publishing dozens of poems each year and entering poetry contests. In these early years, she wrote far more than she published, mainly short lyrics capturing the bliss and pain of love affairs from first consummations to final partings, as in "If I Had Been Less Cautious" or "To a New Lover."

Having become an independent young career woman and poet of some repute in Kansas, and having successfully broken into national and international poetry publications, Babb launched herself upon Los Angeles on the eve of the Great Depression, arriving there only a few months before the stock market crashed on October 24, 1929. Scaling Mt. Lowe shortly after arriving, she pledged in "Conquest" to fling her "wild song [and] have no fears." When her hoped-for job with the *Los Angeles Times* did not materialize, she experienced a period of homelessness and financial insecurity. Undaunted, Babb's poems of that era continued to express her innate zest for life as in "Coute Que Coute" (cost what it may), composed almost a month into the Depression, and "Unholy Grail," also from 1929. Even into her 70s and 80s, Babb's unbridled delight in living fully is reflected in poems like "Search" and the three "Love Songs."

Babb threw herself into her new life in Los Angeles with customary energy, stitching together paid writing gigs and secretarial work, involving herself deeply in left political and writing circles, volunteering, and documenting life in California's migrant camps for the Farm Security

Administration. She continued to write and publish poetry in little magazines even while turning her focus more and more toward prose.

While her earliest poems feature a fluid iambic line and elegant use of figurative language like those of Sidney Lanier, Sara Teasdale, and Edna St. Vincent Millay, whom she admired, Babb slowly moved away from rhymed, metrical verse toward the end of the 1930s in keeping with modern trends in American poetry. Her poems became more image-driven and direct, with a looser, more conversational, line. Two poems on the death of a beloved pet—"To Toby," from 1928, and "Ullalulla," from 1967—illustrate this development. After the mid-1950s, Babb wrote exclusively unrhymed verse, although notations on various typescripts show her experimenting with devices like consonance, repetition, and parallel figures to unify individual poems.

Told in the Seed is inscribed "For Joanne" and, indeed, Babb's agent, confidante, and eventual literary executor Joanne Dearcopp worked closely with her on the selection and finding its publisher, West End Press. This independent press was dedicated to publishing and preserving "people's culture"—it had recently brought out new work by Meridel Le Sueur and boasted a small, but impressive, backlist of multicultural and women writers. That first edition of *Told in the Seed* skews toward Babb's later work. With the exception of "Captive," written in 1932 but never published, the poems date from the second half of her career, from 1955's "Bird of Night" to a slew of poems written and published in the 1990s, including the erotic poems in section VII. These three "Love Songs" and "The Verge" arise from Babb's late-life relationship with an unnamed, much younger "tall brown man" and testify to her delight in "love / wild and sad"—to living life "bold as the bougainvillaea."

The newly selected poems in *Told in the Seed and Selected Poems* comprise Babb's earlier work as well as filling in some gaps in her mature work. From the earliest, one can see themes that mark her oeuvre throughout: poems of love and loss; her empathy with the marginalized and oppressed, whether human or animal; and her deep connection with all the natural world, be it large or small. The poem "Told in the Seed" captures Babb's fascination with seeds as emblems of potential and mystery as well as her abiding sense of connection to the natural world with its bracing solaces and terrors. This abiding interest in seeds can be seen again and again in poems directly addressing seeds and planting, such as

"Giant Sequoia" and "Aristolochia" as well as in those employing seeds more figuratively, such as "This Is the Time and Place to Write a Poem, I Thought," or "Essence." Regardless of theme, one feels Babb's vast appetite for living. The same woman who wrote in a poem published in 1931

Give me all there is of life,
Wormwood and the gall,
Love and beauty, stifling joy—
I would taste it all

wrote in a personal letter to her friend Joanne in 1996, as her health was failing, "I love all kinds of being alive. Every minute!" This zest for life and new experience adds a powerful dimension to her poems. Joy, longing, and sometimes grief commingle in this collection, sometimes in a single poem; and while the formal exigencies of writing poetry soften or restrain emotion, emotion beats, or hums, as Babb would say, just beneath the poem's skin.

An excellent example of such a complex exploration is "Above Malpaso Creek" which takes the occasion of a walk along land owned by Sanora and her husband to reflect on the oppressive burden of history upon the land: the successive people and animals who have walked there, from "soft-footed" cougars to the Spanish conquerors and missionaries and the Indians they enslaved. "No explorers," the speaker and her companion stand on "ground stained and enchanted," which "receives us, warily, aloof," as it has received natives, immigrants, and invaders through the centuries. Fecund and poetic, this same landscape beckons her, via the "knowing gaze" of a mated pair of coyotes, into close communion with its lushly fruiting fig and guava and its amorous creatures, in "34th Parallel: January."

About a third of the poems in the original collection, *Told in the Seed*, had been previously published; the rest were written and rewritten throughout the 1950s-90s. Among the newly selected poems this pattern is reversed: about three quarters of the poems, most of them early, have been previously published. Among the most recent poems in *Told in the Seed* is "Critic" from a special issue of the *Kentucky Poetry Review* dedicated to the life and work of Babb's close friend Ray Bradbury. An example of Babb's subtle wit, the critic-speaker of the poem catalogues a stunning Pacific coastal landscape near Big Sur, with its steep paths and tidal pools, its "chiseled shells" and "amber kelp necklaces / Thrown away by spoiled mermaids," only to note that, "A comma is missing between / The cliff and the yarrows."

Throughout her life, Babb was drawn to outsiders, both human and animal. Evidence of her empathy and identification with marginalized groups and individuals crops up in numerous poems as well as throughout her prose work. Insects, so often despised and overlooked, evoke empathy in Babb, who sees in them an opportunity for mindful coexistence, as in "Spiders" or "Amber." Insects offer a reminder that we humans are both a part of and apart from nature, and that nature's plans do not always include us. Spider, beetle, earthworm, moth: no living creature is too common to be observed, invoked, made room for. This affinity and identification is in part a reflection of her itinerant and impoverished formative years on the Great Plains where her father's gambling isolated the family socially. Her early days of poverty in Los Angeles and her leftist sympathies, too, drew her close to southern California's itinerant worker, labor organizing, and Filipino communities. Her relationship and eventual marriage to James Wong Howe (who experienced both anti-Chinese- and, during the war, anti-Japanese-racism) brought her into further contact with social and institutional racism, as well as with the vibrant Chinese community of Los Angeles.

But it is her childhood relationships with members of the Otoe community of western Oklahoma that feature most vividly in her biographical writing. In particular, her childhood friendship with an Otoe tribal leader left an indelible mark. The earliest published poem in *Told in the Seed*, "Allegro Con Fuoco"—published under that title in *Dalhousie Review* and under the title "I Ride a Wild Horse" in the *University of Kansas City Review*—centers on an exhilarating horseback ride on a pony given her by Chief Black Hawk, a leading figure of the Otoes living near Red Rock. Babb had drawn on this experience in the 1930s, when writing her novel *Whose Names Are Unknown*. She touched on it again in her 1970 memoir, *An Owl on Every Post*. Memories of her old friend, stirred by a magazine photograph of the Otoe leader Old Eagle, are also the genesis of "My Lost Name," which recounts another aspect of that formative childhood ride, when young Sanora earned her Otoe name, "Little Cheyenne Riding Like the Wind." (While this poem about recovering names appears to confuse Black Hawk with the famously photogenic Old Eagle, it should be remembered that in "My Lost Name" Babb was recalling the incident from a distance of almost eighty years.) "One with the Braves" rounds out a trio of poems sprung from her childhood experiences with Native Americans and native culture and cements her sense of oneness with them—"our common breath"—born of long ago "foot races in the red dust / And pony races on the plain."

Among other biographical poems, the grouping "Old Snapshots" also looks back to Babb family life on the Oklahoma panhandle in the early- to mid-1920s, with a focus on small town life. The organizing conceit is the then-new era of casual family photos, made possible by increasingly affordable sturdy compact cameras and amateur-friendly roll film that could be developed by a local druggist or sent to the manufacturer for processing. Captured in these "snapshots" is Babb's father, the charming gambler, sometime baker, and small-town baseball hero Walter Babb. Here too is his long-suffering wife, Jennie Babb, caught in an all-too-brief moment free of domestic drudgery, gazing "tender with regard" at her daughters. Dorothy and Sanora, rich in imagination, each appear in their barren front yard, bursting with potential, seeds of their future selves. When Bernice Slote accepted three of the "Old Snapshots" for Prairie Schooner in 1965 as "good for nostalgia," she cut the Jennie poem—as, so often in her life, Jennie had been eclipsed. Also cut was a fifth poem, about the town's tramp dog "Bakehouse" a consummate individualist who came and went as he pleased and "did not beg." For Told in the Seed, Babb restored Jennie to "Old Snapshots" and added, in section VI, another previously unpublished poem written on her mother's death in 1961, "At Mama's Grave." This collection recovers Bakeshop's "Old Snapshot," along with other poems addressed to beloved dogs, including "Ullalula," and "To Toby."

Babb's husband of almost thirty years, Oscar-winning cinematographer James Wong "Jimmie" Howe, is the subject of four poems mourning his death in 1976: "The Last Year," "A Circling Wind," "Before Sleep," and "Night Visit." Unlike Jennie Babb, who is silent and invisible after death, Jimmie is an active haunting presence, manifesting as a cool, seeking wind, a something sensed beyond a doorway, a phantom hand or pre-dawn embrace. He is present to mind each day as well, in a double-trunked acacia tree or an antique Chinese screen. Living, Howe is a hidden presence in other poems, as in the land that "looks with our eyes, west to the sea / toward Asia" in "Above Malpaso Creek," or in the

"Chinese and Spanish graves" they walk upon in "Night Range of Lions."

"Miranda," composed in 1986, deserves mention as a free-wheeling portrait of the artist at eighty, disguised as a paean to the Uranian moon. An avid reader of news magazines who kept clippings of stories that caught her interest, Babb followed the Voyager II flyby of Uranus closely. She transcribed descriptions of Miranda's odd orbit, incorporating bits into this poem celebrating non-conformity, a salient feature of Babb's personality to the last. Together with "Captive" and "Being," "Miranda" offers Babb's "venturing spirit," one that could never be fully tethered, but sang, soared, wandered, or "wobbled in fun." Consistent with this spirit, "Essence," written when Babb was in her 20s, offered a similarly playful self-portrait of the poet as "a wind . . . Fragrant with swollen seeds" who "will trouble / Your door / And never / Come in." You, the reader, are invited to come in and savor this collection of Sanora Babb's poems.

Carol S. Loranger
2021

I.

Told in the Seed

Tonight I hear the first crickets on the hillside,
A big brown spider sits on my dictionary,
The moon is full, o, moon pulling at my tides.
I know the bees are cold tonight, the spring is uncertain
But flowers are waiting; they have come up
From their secret seeds, no seed confused in its image
No matter how I mix them in the earth,
The worm's fragrant home.
We are strung on the same breath, and this is the secret.
We have not made the deep connection.
This acacia tree with a composition of night birds
Whispers its being, its covenant, and what cannot be said,
Told in the seed; persuaded by sun, sod, the rain and wind,
The lightning and thunder.
I hear the crickets making a song upon the hills.

Aristolochia

This seed delights me.
It is more beautiful than others.
But its beauty is alarming,
Frightening.
I cannot hold back a shiver.
The unknown is close,
The mystery extravagant:
The seed wears the design of its leaf
Drawn on the shell!

Lean Away from the Tree

In the dark I lean against a tree.
I have been warned: Trees are unfriendly at night.
They will comfort you by day.
The spirit of the tree is unknown to you,
As your own: Beware of both after dark.
It is in the pitch of night under the sky,
Susceptible to stars and planets,
Their mystery not yet undone,
That one enters oneness
And being lost in it
Finds the spirit of the seed.
The tree was first,
The fern forest growing and falling in the primal silence.
Remember?
Lean away from the tree. You have been warned.

Why Does the Dog Howl on the Midnight Hill?

Why does the dog howl on the midnight hill,
The architecture of his plaint
Unguarded like a ruin?
What woke him out of sleep
To this gigantic moon?
The monstrous void of thought?
A subtle recognition of his doom?
Has Diana seen him slumbering on the grass
And kissed him as she kissed Endymion
To leave him haunted by one touch of love?
Or did he trail the ghostly stag of time three thousand years
To find that he was Sirius at Orion's heel,
Set in the sky to ornament a huntress' grief?
Why does the dog
With naked solitude engrave the night?
Why does the dog howl on the midnight hill?

Bird of Night

Sleep, sleep, embattled bird of night
Whose splendid wings,
Clipped by the blade of my desire,
Torment the air, whose cumbrous flight
Pounds on the noiseless wall of dark,
Bruising the hours . . .

O bird of prey whose smoky eye
Can't find me now,
O angry bird, be still.
Enfold me in your sleep-black wings,
Binding my imaged sight.

Deceive me with a fury of delight!

Allegro con Fuoco

I ride a runaway horse—
Hooves, pulse of wakened stones,
Mane combed by wind,
Ears back, eyes fire,
Heart wild,
And thighs all quiver.
Tail streaking air
Like a broken star.
We flash on a plain of dark:
One lightning in one summer storm,
In atomed days
Of dreamless dust
To store this gloried flight.

II.

Old Snapshots

I

A panhandle town in Oklahoma
North of the Texas line,
An old house in back—paint cut to the board
Bared to the hot sunshine.
A clothesline propped by a forked cedar post,
A dog pants in the shade,
A girl poses in an elegant dress
You'd never know she made;
She leans on a thin, graceful walking stick:
Paris' newest new fad.
The weed grown path was the Rue de la Paix:
Such were the dreams I had!

II

Little sister and friends sit in the shade
Of sage brush on the sand,
Bandanaed, beaded, bangled, full-skirted,
A wily gypsy band.
One tells a fortune with playing cards spread,
One reads the God-marked hand,
One fills a false pocket to supplement
Chance: to live off the land.
The wind blows their garments, drouth scars the field
Poverty on their shoes;
Eyes signal riches of spirit and coin,
Journeys, go along, blues.

III

Sunday afternoon inside the drugstore
After the baseball game,

19

Papa, the hero circled by his team:
Pitcher of bush-league fame.
Marble-topped tables, vanilla ice cream,
Cool green-rivers in glass;
The fountain is swamped, sun beats on the town;
Players are served first class.
Papa looks handsome (he had Irish charm),
Even with sweat-limp hair;
Worshipful girls in voile and organdy
Lean on cases and stare.
Diamond runners from store, farm and office,
By weekday commonplace,
Transformed by Sunday's baseball game, smile back
With a hero's face.

IV

Home from a journey to Kansas City:
In chic suit, georgette blouse,
Mama's black velvet hat trimmed with real jet
Looks too fine for our house.
Her little feet in twenty dollar shoes
Stand on the hard bare yard;
Her face lightly powdered with Cara Nome
And tender with regard
For daughters taking her pretty picture
As she came from the train,
Before in apron and flat-heeled slippers,
Housewifery makes her plain.

III.

Recognition's Glance

Leaves, brother of mineral,
Flesh, sister of stone,
Sun, father of breath:

Dust of dinosaur and redwood
Of fishbone and daisy,
Of snake and wolf,
Small lizard mingled
With the goat's pale hair:
Of lark's still wing,
Cicada's song
And sires of Sophocles,
Of mouse, and leopard's grace
And hawk's dissolving eye;
Of cuckoo egg in alien nest
And sleeping bees,
Of fossilled love
Sequent in midnight forest
Or daylight's sweet approval;
Of turquoise bones,
Of ancient rains,
Tomorrow's wind:
All these are we, and more,
All rich reality
Combined and traveled down
The seasons of the universe
To make a child, a poem,
A painting, music and
A living stone. . . .

And so
Not less than these,
One flower of mind's long history
Of leaf and rock and sun:
The speech of eyes, time's idiom—
The immortality
Of recognition's glance.

Wedding Song

Go, stranger, into my garden,
Taste the young May herbs,
Herbs from the Orient
Seeded in times of trouble;
Stand in the stream of wind
Scented with mock orange
And leaf of mint
Crushed in the night
By the fox's toe.
I know him better
Than you-and-me together:
He has no words to cover his essence
As we have to explain and conceal.

The day is veiled and tender,
Yet, so clear under the sky that I see
The white-walled, tile-roofed city
On the valley floor,
And beyond the pock-marked land
To the whale back of Catalina in the sea.
But we are impeded by casuality.
A house wren trills from his elegant Spanish door:
A vent in the wall.

The midnight dog howls
At three o'clock in the afternoon.
The eucalyptus swaying in slow grace
Matches the rhythm of my tides,
And, bemused that I am sister

To this worm measuring a leaf,
I learn that knowing
Travels tortuous ways by timeless clocks
That tick in nowhere.

Go, stranger, into my garden
Where the day's sweet emanations
Are understood by birds and trees,
And see if you can find me
In the multiple singing air.
Go there, because I cannot look into your eyes,
Myself a stranger aware of you
Unguarding your guarded dream.

Santa Cruz

We rejected the glass motel on the rocky coast
Where open windows blended the salt air
With the fragrance of rare redwood forests;
The white pier, the white Ferris wheel,
The caged carousel with bright horses a century old
Being too near. These and the ugly people.
On spindly balconies the ugly people bulged
In their burned skin and gaudy towels.
He saw them and wanted a quiet place. I, too.
But I saw the place as it began, its clean walk
Touched by the long embroidered skirts of women
Carrying parasols above their flowery hats,
Husbands at ease smoking long cigars,
Children high-spinning or galloping
In fantasy's wild and secret place.
I saw them all from old books I had read,
Those genteel people from another time
Come to the seashore (not the beach)
To calm their fevers in a calmer year.
I saw the flaccid, mammalian couples
Superfatted, nerves lashed in the hurricane's eye,
Seeking that same elemental sun and air and peace,
Strained through the soil of an advancing human race.

Giant Sequoia

I am in awe of this small seed,
Its perfect design and the design within:
The great sequoia tree sleeping, waiting
To send down its first root
No bigger than an eyelash.
The parent tree stands near,
Its fluted bark defying malady and fire,
Its body embracing a river of sap
Flowing upward to a pollen-yellowed crown
Known only to flying things, to sun and storm.
Here, far below, roots graze through acres
Of true, sustaining earth.
While ages were rising and blooming and dying,
While man was going his tender, learning, savage
And fragile way,
This tree was growing—
In snows of the unnamed Sierra Nevadas
And ancient, nameless Pacific winds,
Aloof in this dusky grove,
Its life begun two thousand years
Before Christ was born.

Critic

At the witching hour
I went alone down the steep path
To the Pacific shore,
All trembling, all eager,
And found that it was
Low tide, with one carp.

There among the bruised
And chiseled shells,
The amber kelp necklaces
Thrown away by spoiled mermaids;
There beside the poor dead fish,
The one carp, something was missing.
I knew it with my finest sense,
And yet, how tell it
and not offend the creator?

Be bold! I cried. "Be bold!"
Echoes along the Big Sur.
A comma is missing between
The cliff and the yarrows.

Above Malpaso Creek

Our land looks, with our eyes, west to the sea
Toward Asia; waves beat an ancestral pulse
That echoes briefly in our blood.

Our land looks northward to a cypress grove
Green from a mountain spring and shaped by wind
Blowing through Indian memories.

Our land looks south to the hidden Big Sur,
Canyons and creeks, hills and redwoods between.
The stirring grasses speak in tongues.

We look east to the Santa Lucias;
Deer sleep in the heather and cougars go
Soft-footed in the dark watching

Our ways. Malpaso, evil passage, mocks
Our glad, naive delight, and haunts the sun.
The dog growls at the peopled air.

In 1542 Cabrillo looked
Upon this coast. Two hundred years ago
Portola chanced this wilderness.

And Father Junipero built
Great Spanish missions forcing Indian hands;
The Indians, offered cross or sword,

Were gathered, enslaved, to newer gods that
In the name of light brought dark. Mexico
Freed them to payless peonage.

This ground stained and enchanted, hints its past
Though only feral feet disturb it now.
The Spaniards left their singing names.

But, no explorers, we, we'll leave no name:
The land receives us warily, aloof,
Its grandeur stern, its primitive wild heart

Isolate and proud. We walk respectful,
Offering our love. The wind blows over
This lonely place, alluding to phantoms,

Implying presences from other years,
And running, resplendent horses flashing
Silver buckles; and wild things unafraid.

No voice says yes, but none says no.
We offer our love to the living wind,
To sea, to earth, to animals and birds,

Insects and worms, grass and flowers and trees.
We mention the sun, the moon, and the stars.
We praise the universe, our joining breath.

The land is mute but eloquent. We stay,
Aware that we invade this timeless space
Made virginal again by the lost years.

Night Range of Lions

This windy headland
Above the western sea,
Backed by the Santa Lucias,
This land of strong, coarse grass and heather
Where deer sleep in the afternoons
And whales go by,
Place of sea wind and silent ground
And canyon mysteries,
Night range of lions,
This unrevealing turf a century
Upon Chinese and Spanish graves . . .
We walk here, it is ours.
But under the wind the hooves echo;
In the clear air, the naked horsemen ride by.
When they have gone (before they came),
This lone windy place speaks only
Of a sentient time when no man was.

IV.

The Last Year

The tree you planted years ago
Grew in two strong trunks
Joined near the earth:
Our lives, you said,
The trunks branched wide and full,
Leaves and yellow flowers shaded
A place we kept for birds,
Water and grain.
A window where we sat watching
Wings glide down to sanctuary.
I sit here now.
The acacia trunks have aged,
Furrows dent their roundness,
Sap runs low,
But old scars, grey eyes on grey bark,
See my tears as they saw your own
Kept secret from me—you thought—
When the days left were only a few.
You longed to be with the growing,
Not the dying, so you lay in the sun
And the wind where every tree
Spoke in its way of moving,
And white clouds drifted that the sky
Would be bluer for your hungering gaze.
We held hands, our love more eloquent
Than in the passions of our youth
That cannot know how deep the roots,

How high old branches range the air,
How beautiful love is full of years.
All seasons we grew in tenderness and strife.
The symmetry now broken.

A Circling Wind

Here is your Chinese screen from an ancient dynasty,
People with ivory faces and jade gowns
In the tea house made of semi-precious stones,
Shaded by maple and pine trees with jade leaves.
Children play at ancient games that children play today.
Girls cross a bridge as beautiful as they, all jewels.
The Eight Legendary Horses cavort above them all,
Jade, pink quartz, mother-of-pearl and red carnelian.
The lacquered edges curl a little with a thousand years of time
And still they are intact.

I tell myself your spirit lives,
And you have spoken to me in the way of shades:
Your love and comfort in a cool and tender wind
That circled round me close and closer still.
You knew I like the wind, its livingness.
Was it a signal from your life to prove life has no end?

This screen, a thing of beauty, made by man,
Is not a man, and yet you both endure.
The wood and you who had a name will turn to ash,
Perhaps to jewels some other day.
The light that looked at me from your dark eyes
Is like the wind that circles me, the sweet round wind,
The you that is you.
The you with a name is gone, and for him I grieve.

Before Sleep

Before I sleep I stand at the door
Looking down on the city, its diamonds
In curving rows for all the world as if
The stars have fallen down.
The western sky is big over the wide valley.
It meets the sea like the lid of a box closing
Over jewels. Small diamonds gleam on the sea
And wink in the air. A ruby bracelet circles a tower.

You stood here, and I knew you were thinking
Is this the last night I look down from the hills
On my city? Where I have for so many years
Made images that secured my name,
A perishable name in a mutable world.

I stand at the same door before I sleep.
Books, accumulating, weigh half the bed.
I watch the patterned stars in the dark sky
And the half-moon as desolate as I.

Night Visit

When you live alone in a house in a canyon
Among dark forested mountain walls,
You do not expect to be awakened at 3 A.M.
By an arm around your body just under your breasts
With a hand seeking your hand.
You do not move, you hold your breath in terror.
Then, for sanity, for desperate confirmation
That this is a dream,
Your hand touches. *Real!*

If this is my destiny, cruel in the guise of love,
I must see its stranger's face,
Be sudden in lesser strength
And use my cunning to escape.
I turn: The arm, as alone as I, lifts tenderly.
Your hand as familiar to me as my own
Smooths away my fear.
This was as much as your uncaged spirit
Could manifest this time, as much perhaps
As my mortal heart could bear.
If you can come to me again from that far place,
(Or is it here pulsing too fine a beat
For our bound senses to understand?)
If you should come to me again saying your love,
Come to me in a dream and speak my name.
I will open an ancient door in my mind.
And walk into that dream.

Puzzle

In the cold regions of the universe
Purported to be alight with an inner flame
Visible only to the third eye
Lives a self-existent, abstract artist
Who is mathematician, engineer, magician,
Soothsayer, o, all things known and unknown,
Who, among a great many other creativities,
Perhaps just to while away the timelessness,
Makes pristine souls (that grow old in the shuttle),
Moves them about in groups and frees them
Into corruption and grace, as they choose. Mainly,
They choose a little of each, but some go
To extremes and take one or the other.
Either way they have a long way to go,
More lives to live,
In order to reach understanding, a foreign country
Even though it is really home.
This magician, magic in the true sense, no charlatan,
This magician whose twinkling of an eye is an aeon,
Watches these souls for centuries at a time.
Some say with love, some with benevolent humor.
Others with irony. Who is to say? We are lacking,
Having been let loose with only our senses
As learning tools with the mysterious inner injunction
(Especially urgent when looking into the night sky
Or being with flowers and trees, or a seed,
All such profound and simple things)
With the injunction to know ourselves,
To discover our souls, our souls that remember

And send little sparks of large longing
(Sublime restlessness, old poets called it)
That glorify our stumbling, dancing days.
Like all else, the amateur souls have their seasons,
Shedding their skins like snakes,
Taking new roles in their circle
Like actors in a repertory: the spear-carrier
May be king, the king a grave-digger,
All with new lessons to learn,
Dismayed by cause and effect of their own doing.
But determined, enduring, humble and arrogant, divinely sparked.

How many roles have you and I played in our cosmic cell?
How many and various affinities have we shared
To come to this one indivisible?
Apart again, still a long journey to go
Over symbolic deserts, cruel ravines,
Beautiful mountain meadows and city streets.
Shall we pass in a crowded street one day,
Seeming strangers,
Our eyes in sudden exchange of recognition and memory,
So deep and mystifying it haunts the rest of our years?

V.

In a Field in Peloponesia

In a strange country on a strange hill,
I lean on a wind blowing from Damascus
Or Cairo or even Tripoli.
It does not matter. What matters is
That I stand in a place I've never seen before
Looking down upon the blue Aegean Sea,
And all, all, everything, the baked earth,
The small rocks at my feet, the olive tree,
The wind, and beyond, over a Peloponesian hill,
My whitewashed home I have never seen
But know is there.
In this old land I am an alien, yet
I turn to climb the stony path
To a familiar place I cannot know.

Night in a Greek Village

The bicyclers have gone home and
One horse-drawn buggy rustles on the shore road;
In a little café on the quay
Late table-sitters caress their resin wine
Over a bowl of water floating new peaches.
Two strong old men drink black coffee,
Seasoning their talk of fish and atomic disquietude
With the names of pagan gods.
Dark has risen from the miniature harbor
High, high but the sky is pushing it back.
I walk into the long evening silence,
Into the syllables of summer,
Past an unfinished boat left safe near the water,
The gentle water lapping at the pebbled shore
Where moonlight casts wet shadows on the stays.
The village is a labyrinth of hilly paths,
Old houses, simple, small, solid on the rock-rough land.
Lamplit windows are shy against the night.
A woman is sitting alone on a doorstep.
Stillness. Stillness. The paths branch and cross.
Suddenly a burst of singing farther up the hill:
Boys' voices yearning and joyous, bold with being.
A flame jumps into the dusk, and girls are laughing
And running and leaping over the fire
In an ancient fertility rite. I remember now
The flower wreaths over the doors.
Silence again, darkness, the moon drowning in the Aegean.
Black night, black, black, the lamps are out.
Only the water sparkled by the stars to lead me home.

The paths are lost in the fields of night,
Paths that at dusk had moved me with their unknown stories:
Paths are alike all over the world.
At last I go along the rocks to the Greek house where I live,
The house with the icon over the door,
With a pot of basil on the porch rail
That the Greeks tousle as they go by;
The clean, sparse room of table and bed. My books.
I lean from the window looking into the visible dark,
At the darker shapes of the village.
I hear the quarter-hour bell in the church,
The strange bird with its single note;
I hear the years of this island's life
In the clean air of its silence, in the bird call,
In the sudden evening trouble of
A child sickened by the evil eye.
I listen to the tideless night and the tideless sea,
I am lost in the special loneliness of islands.

VI.

At Mama's Grave

Is she here, deaf in her satin bed of sometime dust?
Does she stand aside one with the wind and the roses
Barriered to silence by our ignorance?
When the key turned, was the door closed or opened?
What is death? What is life? Are they one?
By the fence the red roses for love that nod loving
Know beyond question, know more than we.
That voice in the mockingbird song: is it she?
All one, the sky says, the earth says, my heart says,
Then, let her be.

Night

The night listens;
Language is undone,
Thoughts translate
To pure meaning.

The Visitor

Safe in the light, walled against the lion and the thief,
Lulled by the evening rite of women in ancient rhythms
Of the meal, forming the unformed into an offering of love.
She moves enclosed in the work without dream, unwary
Of the windowed dark and the dark's great company
Crowding the air, weightless on flowers, unpierced by thorns,
Unhindered by matter spun from motion, their easy element.
Is the grass startled by their amorphous feet?
Do the trees shudder in the cosmic winter's cold?
Or, by the strange intelligence of other living things,
Accept?
What being defies the lock, flows past, makes for the stair
Unseen, unheard, raising the fine hairs of her arms
And bristling the dog's hackles? His eyes focus on the empty air.

L'Immortelle

Taken from earth I touch like the wind
Once and forever, this dust I hold
In reverence so small, once other life,
Will be again.

Impenetrable now it lies:
A mystery of planetary years
Hid in its common grain.

But heart, related with the wondering mind
By sense at first and science after,
Perceives its ordered change—
 In nights on plain and hill, aware
Of brief nobilities of question
And connection with the changing all,
Feels histories of primal rise;
Endures griefs infinite as cosmos
And revives.

So, importunes the wisdom of an unknown star,
Hears voice as real as mist that once was rain:
A cry of longing drifted through
The wilderness of suns:
Some other planet's lover's loneliness,
Some other artist's gift fulfilled, betrayed.

All this I hold, too small to see,
Too vast to understand
Except by the dust that I have been

Blown off the shores of dissipated seas,
Become this self, intuitive of:
In other time and place,
This need
Which reassembled now in me
Burns to my roots uncounted ages growing,
Filling me not with one man's love
And one man's thought,
And one man's bold creative dream—
But with the complex fragments
Of a multitude of minds
Dissolved and scattered
On the universal fields
Shaped once again in me.

VII.

34th Parallel: January

In this winterless land
New grass is already green
On the rough western hills

Two crows dispute on a cypress
And singing birds ornament the air
And the heart with joy

Yellow mimosa flowers tremble
Like new love

Silently fig and guava trees
Create their fruit for summer

Dove gallants bow and beseech
Pretend-indifferent-alluring mates

Two handsome coyotes paired for life
Come down the mountain at dawn and dusk
And give me the pleasure of their knowing gaze

Spring tries to assert its being
In lyric ways unknown to the single season.

Love Song I

My tall man
My tall brown man
At work on the hills
In the sun,
Singing and working.
Across a canyon
Rough with chaparral
We see each other . . .
Too far to speak.
Bold as the bougainvillaea
Gripped in a rage of bloom,
We send our message
Whose primal power
Stuns our minds and
Burns the air.
Help us, cool will,
To break the spell
And banish us back to work
And exile.

Love Song II

My tall man
My tall brown man
Whose name sings
In an old oppressor's tongue,
Whose blood runs deep
In ancient Indian springs . . .
Who are you to me?
And I to you?
We are enigmas.
Our nerves ache with love
Wild and sad,
Our bodies blend
In renewing fire,
Our ways are apart,
Our thoughts shared mysteries.
Who are you to me
And I to you?
Shall we remember this longing?
Or shall we honor
The heart's changing weathers
In new times of love?
Let us go on
In the secret and shining dark
And not beware.

The Verge

We swim in rhythmic waters
In the sacred lake of being,
Immersed in magic
We seek to reveal.

We love. Oneness is given
And withdrawn.
Overwhelmed, the secret knowledge
Dissolves in pure awareness.

Alight in the dark,
Unrelated to all others,
We are on the verge
Of the only secret there is.

Love Song III

My tall man
My tall brown man
Of silences.
In love, act or eyes
Are enough.
We talk too much.
A river flowing in a song,
A tree joyous with birds waking,
Bells ringing over the owl's omen
Say his love is long
And rooted in the earth of our hearts,
The earth old, old with the bodies
Of time's used beings,
New and alive with the silent unknown,
Unmasked in the sun's heat,
Sealed again in the cool moon's shine.
My tall man, may you walk
In the company of your shadow,
Pondering now and then
A certain small splendor.

Summer Dark

Tonight a sickle moon
And its fabled star.

The mountain is black,
Its hidden night life
Waking in the brush . . .
Small legs and wings make music
In mighty waves and swells,
A thousand million insects
Celebrate
The summer dark.

I am longing for my lover.

Echo

When I was remembering you
A year after you'd gone,
I surprised myself,
As the saying goes:
You and I were walking side by side
Across the garden,
You were pressing your case,
As the saying goes:
You said, I can wait.

I relive the later embraces,
All the heady joy,
But what comes back so tenderly:
Our slow walking together
And your saying,
I can wait.

Again

I keep remembering someone I do not know:
I dreamed about you before we met:
We were in an arid place in another time,
You were mending a corral to hold our horses,
I at the door of an adobe house, watching you,
Love flowing between us like the rhythms of earth.

Again our love is new,
Rich with ecstasy and discovery and an old sorrow.

You came a stranger, after the dream,
And I knew you in an unknown way.
You knew me first.
You were importunate,
You overcame my wary remembrance.
New time seized hold of an old thread of longing
And we were happy again,
As close as the veins of leaves
As lyric as larks
As destined as seeds

As mortal as pulse.
Years and borders
Separate us. Again,
In the quick of love.

Whoever we are next time
You will know me
And I will know you, as if
Remembering someone I never knew.

Silence

In a subtle wind from the south
I hear your silence
And the words in that silence
Hidden like seeds in a pod
Ripening to scatter on the wind,
To find and fall into my heart,
To be understood in my being,
To answer you as voiceless as
Night stars speak their ancient tongue
From the vast cold dark of no boundaries
To your listening wherever you are.

VIII.

Captive

When I am old, and young mouths say that spring
Has ceased to work her alchemy with me:
That white thorn boughs and apple trees in bloom
Stir me no more . . . that I no longer see
The courage of a fledgling taking wing . . .
And soft nights cause no ache in my old breast,
They will not know that laughter at a gate
Will break my heart with memories—oh! lest
I make some commonplace remark and go
Where scent of spring and footsteps on the grass
Are shut outside . . . and where there is no room
For shadows of a gay young man to pass . . .
And never will they guess my feeble pulse
Still throbs at beauty and exhausts me quite,
Who, though I sit at dusk alone and still,
Have sent my venturing soul far in the night.

Being

I am like larks
                    all singing
Singing   flying upward   singing
Rising   rising
I am like doves
at evening   mourning
Bleak   and single
Calling   calling   calling
I am like common sparrows
in rain   yielding
But in morning   waking   shaking
Newly joyous   singing   soaring
Singing!

IX.

Miranda

I am in love with Miranda.
She is a free spirit.
How she escapes the celestial rules
Is a mystery not even science understands.
She whirls the opposite of Nature's whirls,
Lurching, tumbling: it's called erratic orbit.
She even wobbles in fun sometimes,
That is, for millions of years,
And wanders on impulse.

Miranda is a little planet, a little moon
Of Uranus, just three hundred miles across,
A good day's drive, but rough
Over "cliffs, craters and oddly stacked terraces."
She lives among the stars, too small
To shine in Earth's far sight,
But her non-conformist ways
Puzzle the searcher's mind
And nudge his heart.

X.

I Thought I Saw the Dawn Go By

I thought I saw the dawn go by
A-racing for the town;
She still had blue night in her hair
And wore a saffron gown.

I thought I caught a sideways glimpse
Of stardust in her eyes
And cloud mist on her cheek that hid
A sleepy shy surprise—
But then the sun rolled from the hill
And left me wondering about her still.

The Restive Plains

There is peace in the hill country
Where the horizon,
Rolled by streams and trees,
Shuts the heart in . . .
Where a browsing mountain
Presses bluntly against the sky,
Admitting no dreams of the land
On its lee.

But on the plains there is no peace—
Plains—where violent clouds lie down
And lightning reaches fiery arms
To seek their calm . . .
Where the far smooth worldline,
Swept back by virile winds
Beyond the trembling mirages
That suggest silvered Utopias,
Stretches the pain-wise soul
To aching point
To touch infinity.

Kansas Prairie

I have lived where the hills rolled the skyline
Too close to the edge of the town,
I have lived where the tall steel man-made towers
Cut the horizon, and found
That my spirit hungered for miles of clear view
Instead of mountains that I hoped to see through—
A tan grass prairie, a Kansas plain,
With wind that asked for a drink of rain,
That stretched with freedom and rolling ease
To the end of the sky, unmarked with trees.

Rain

Day after day my footsteps trace
Themselves along this selfsame street.
Night after night I read my books,
Or count my eager pulse's beat.

I watch the sun wheel by a day
And set behind a brackened hill.
I seek a place of lights to find
That people make me lonelier still.

On certain nights the moon is hung
Above a solitary palm—
Such aching beauty binds my lips
That fashion words to plea for calm.

Tonight the rain, soft like moth wings,
Dropped crystals in my hair, and paved
The asphalt thick with liquid stars
Where lay bright tracks silver engraved.

Whether it sooths my restive will
Or gently stirs a dormant fire,
Rain against my cheek is ecstasy,
And sweet to know as first desire.

Fog

Tonight when the fog stole in
On soft gray paws
And hovered over city streets,
Creeping noiselessly into valleys,
Shunning the heights,
While a thousand lights pushed gently
Through the sifting mist,
Beauty-blind and lonely-wise,
I pressed through its pliable walls,
Conscious of restraining fingers
Moist against my cheek.
Steep ascent. And pause . . . now only
Braver lights thrust up their glistening shafts.
What if every timid gleam below
Yields to the bland body of the fog!
I could not be more lonely
Here in this cool embrace,
Remembering
That so short a time ago
I looked at all this splendor . . .
Half-eager, half-afraid that you would hear
The throbbing of my pulse for you
And answer it,
Leaving me lonelier than I was before.

Today

Today,
Outlines are sharp
Against the fog . . .
Houses on the landscape
Look like toy castles
On a cardboard hill . . .
Tall eucalyptus trees
Along the slopes
Fringe their peaks
Like paper cut-outs
Pasted on
A wet mauve sky.

I Had Forgotten

I had forgotten how a winter moon
Hung in a cold clear sky,
How a star could leave a silver trail
Against the blue to die,
How the bare uncanny branches
Stood out white and still
Against the mounting purple vault
Like tombs on an aged hill;
I had forgotten somehow where to find
Calm and beauty and rest—
Till I stood here, alone, remembering
You like the winter best.

Measure

Perhaps some dreamer knows
This grimy laborer touches infinity
When he raises a towering edifice
Out of a labyrinth
Of wood and steel and stone.
But I would not weigh him down
With dreamers' thoughts.
He may rise at dawn,
Tacitly rejoice in breathing morning air
Unstenched by smoke and men,
He may make beauty against the sky
With cold and ugly tools,
He may sweat at his work,
And curse, or he may not curse,
He may go home to simple pleasures,
He may feel pride
To build a massive work . . .
But . . . can it be a thing
Like feeling aching chords of music
Or the catch of breath
At a bird's swift flying?

It Is the Way the Deep Lush Grass

It is the way the deep lush grass
Roots bravely to the precipice edge,
The way the wind mourns over the low bleak hills
And blows into the sea,
The way the rain drives over the downs
Staining the trees and shining the low stone walls
The way a mockingbird sings his hesitant copied notes
Before the rain . . . the notes breaking sharply
Over the white rock cliffs that march along
The sea.
The way these quiet, lonely country sounds
Come into me, that turns my heart's anger
Into an upthrust fist, as the army planes
Roar over, startling the sheep a little,
Waking the shepherd hardly, raising his head;
It is expected, yet unbelieved, that bombs
Will drop on London, a few hours away,
That gas will tear a choked and ragged strip
Of death through England.
The radio, the newsreel and the press show
The death-head muzzle of the twentieth century man:
The government makes them now: 11 million people
Wait and doubt, believe and unbelieve the fears
That burn in their minds at night,
When they hear the monotonous roar of the surf
Hurled back to itself by the mighty roar
Of a bomber squadron rehearsing death.

This Is the Time and Place to Write a Poem, I Thought

This is the time and place to write a poem, I thought.
But why? When I cannot say
What the moist earth is humming into the skin of my bare feet,
The grass singing a green song around my ankles
And now my knees pressed to the cushion of tear moss
Feel the long slow tides of the sea like breath in the summer land;
My hands in the fragrant earth rich with dead leaves,
My hand placing a seed in full knowing what its flower and fruit
In a little time, compared to aeons, will be.
I can wait, as I wait for the peaches above me to grow
As the tree grew from a seed I dropped there
Not too many years ago.
I am of earth, the elements of my flesh the same,
But there is still the mystery, undisclosed, of the spirit and mind
That lets this seed grow,
This egg be bird and singing,
These white moths whirl in the eternal dance of twos,
This flower give its scent
For which our word is no definition;
That lets the walls of this canyon pulse like our blood
Beneath its rough flesh of old granite, now soil,
Whiskered with chaparral and trees: jacaranda, eucalyptus, and pepper
Each moving in its own rhythm to the unseen wind,
To the unseen.

XI.

To Some Visiting Birds from the North

You do not come as robins come
To notify of season,
But fill my trees, as travelers pass
Through foreign stations and walk
A moment up and down beside the train
To breathe the foreign air; so you
Fly up and down my hill, chirping like
Giddy tourists, sampling this berry
And that fruit, and no doubt
Making comment that tropic climes
Are wine-like and colors on a spree,
But how do birds whose home this is
Endure year-round ennui?

Infidelity

For hours, then days
The thrush in his fine feathers
Flirts and struts and drops his wings
And bows to himself
In the gleaming metal hubcap
Of an automobile at the curb—
In love, enamored,
Bewitched as never before,
Pecked by his mate
Who sees the reflection
For what it is and is twice-jealous
Of her bird twice-fooled.
She waits on the wire above
For him who thinks he is misunderstood,
Who joins her when his mirror and his love
Roll away
Leaving him lost to himself
And regained to his hen
Who unlike the aping reflection
Pecks him again and flies away
To a nearby tree
And a half-built nest.
He follows, matured,
Making the first compromise
Of his free-flying life.

Ullalulla

For Chico

Days were brighter than noon,
Nights were sweet and tender with his sleep,
All hours impressed our living
With his need and gift of love.
He leaped with animal poetry
And his eyes sang spirit and soul,
Or flared with savage jealousy
To possess his own.
His being was in the very texture
Of our sun to sun of years,
Our dark sparkled with the stars
Of his delight. He was of many ways
And yet the sum was joy.
A bird flew past the window,
A bird so wide of wing and black
We ran outside to see him disappear
Into the air before our sight.
Marauding owl or omen?
How empty, silent, lonely
With him gone.

To Toby

Nothing marks his little grave
But a smooth fresh heap,
No one knows about his leaving,
No one knows the grief I keep;
Silently I mourn and want him,
Think of things he did and knew—
How he cheered me, how he loved me,
Little dog, I think of you.

Fire Cat

Imperturbable, impenetrable
The cat sits in the fire
With nose smug, and
Criticizing eyes half-closed
Against me;
Eyebrows of flame
That glow and fade
To signal the temper
Of his advice without words
That claims an orderly wisdom
Far beyond me
Who cannot sit imperturbable
In the burning fire.

Birds in a Storm

The birds were waiting for me;
They expected me at nine and four.
It was now four-thirty and they had not seen me all day.
They had their own clocks.
The hard rain slanted down, beating, flooding;
It roared down the hill street and over the curb.
Lightning cracked the cloud-dark sky
And thunder shook the city.
In the hushed intervals I heard the birds.
People rushed home through the storm,
Their cars slashing great sheets of water.
I went to the high place where I fed the birds.
When they saw me they chattered and sang
And flew out of the sheltering trees,
Landing thick on the ground, turning it their colors.
I gave them days of seed.
The rain beat on me and hurt me,
It came down like a solid blow.
It threw its strength upon the birds.
They accepted it, they ate and chattered.
A few were staggered.
One of them flew up onto a red roof tile
And sang a whole melodic tumble of notes
Before flying back into a streaming, wind-shaken tree.

Spiders

In the rainy season spiders appear
As if in migration, or resettling.
They like especially my workroom
Where books and manuscripts
Provide arbors and darkness.
When I turn on the light they run,
Escaping as if I am after them.
But I am not.
I move carefully in order
Not to hurt or molest one
(I have heard they bite if molested
And that the brown house spider is now known
To be as poisonous as the black widow.)
All are here.
You have all become house spiders
In this season.
I haven't the heart to interfere
With whatever native course or planless plan
Has brought you.
Do not consider my writing a molestation;
There are enough papers and books
And dark unknown corners for us all.

Amber

It is the season of the fig beetle
They look like they rode
A hot Sahara wind straight from Egypt
Their scarab bodies buzz and glide
Like small planes
Landing on their namesake fruit
There they cluster like green jewels
Whiling away the hours sucking fig juice
Their iridescent green
The same green in your eyes
The color closest to the pupil
That fathomless heaven-dark spot
Ever changing in size
Black- to fig beetle green- to golden

Bastet outdid herself
Designing your eyes
You were her child
Daughter of the Sun
Regal under lampshade crowns
Resting your silken chin
On window sill crystals
Or following the sunlight's
Slow migration across the floor
Curled up and basking in its warmth
Like an Egyptian Goddess

I miss you

Last night as I climbed the stairs
A huge bat-sized moth
Flew out of the fig tree
To light on the Rose geranium
In front of my door
The eye-like markings on its wings
Reflecting dim in the new Moon's light
How like you I thought
To send a creature of such dark beauty
To terrify and tantalize
And tell me of your transformation
And that all is well with you

The fig beetle will die too
Drunk on fig juice
They will drop like ripened fruit
And with Autumn they will transmute
Under the fig tree
To iridescent dust
To return again
As will you sweet spirit
Someday
With the warm summer sun

XII.

Coute Que Coute

I am weary of much hearing
What people have to say
Of wanting cake and eating it
And letting come what may.

If I keep it in the cupboard
It will grow stale untouched.
I'll be too old to care for sweets
My hands have never clutched.

I shall eat my cake and care not
About the hungry days.
I may find more; if not, I shall
Walk wisely down lean ways.

For My Inquisitive Friends

Give me all there is of life,
Wormwood and the gall,
Love and beauty, stifling joy—
I would taste it all.

Doubtful friends I have, and foes
Busy with my sin,
They who sip at life and know
Naught of me within.

Conquest

I, of the prairies, have conquered a mountain,
I, who have shunned the deep echo of hills,
Fearing my song flung out always carelessly,
Would return swiftly with vengeance that kills.

Here on the stoic breast of a sage mountain,
Echoes run deeply and finding no ears,
Lose themselves utterly . . . surely . . . inextricably . . .
I fling this wild song, and I have no fears.

Poem

No longer do I
Pick the hours
Like red wild plums
From the green bush,
Nor do I
Lean them
Neat and smug
In little rows
Against the wall
Of my days.
I have no need for plan nor pattern
Anymore.
I have a note in music
To blow through
The curtains
Of the year
Like a swift wild creature
Through the pathless ways
Of night.
I have a note in music
On which to string
The hours
The days
And blow them
Like a swift thing
Through the horn
Of my love
Through the pathless year.

Unholy Grail

Though I break bread at many boards
And drink of many wines,
No time will I be free of want,
Nor are there any signs

That beauty is enough for me,
Nor love, nor all the rest
Of life, nor your dear weight upon
My eager, answering breast.

But I shall seek the enigma out,
My questing lot is cast . . .
Hunger and thirst I'll always know
Unto the very last.

Search

At night I go unguarded
Amid the ruins of other midnights,
Rejecting the path between the rocks
That bruised me on the first journey.
In the dark I wish for the moon of intuition
To magnetize my tides,
To set in motion the rhythm
And crash new words
Upon this stubborn, implacable shore.

I go unguarded,
No beast will harm me,
Unafraid except of man
Who waits, not waiting,
Hidden, not hiding,
Beyond the glass door shielding
The mortal lightning of quick decision
That can still strike me
After my long journey
To bring new words
From the excavated ruins.

Plea

Oh, let me die before my senses stand
Immune to these—the mystery of one new
Rolled leaf, the loneliness of winter trees,
The awesome majesty of storms, the song
In forlorn wandering winds; oh, let me die
Before my scorn of young lovers begins.

For Future Reference

If I must lie within a grave
Dug from a measured plot of ground,
The customary six by three,
With tombstones grinning all around,
Let there be nothing else to crowd
My body tense for final rest,
For I have loved above all things
The tang of mellow, dark earth best.
My dust will take too long to settle
If I must lie in silk and metal.

XIII.

One with the Braves

Days before powwows
We walked the river banks,
Searching for eagle feathers
Under pecan trees.
The many-feathered headdress
Was not ours to wear.
Beaded bands with one power feather
Gave us an air
For foot-races in the red dust
And pony races on the plain.
All Otoe winners, one with the eagle,
The hot sun and the wind,
One with our horses, the hoof-beaten road,
One with the air of our common breath,
One with the braves.

My Lost Name

In a magazine a picture of Old Eagle,
Bear claws, symbol of power and rank, and beads
Framing his Lincoln medal,
Opened a door closed on memory
Of my name. The Otoe chief of my childhood,
Revered Old Eagle.
He gave me a pinto pony, set me on bareback,
Gave him a gentle pat to walk.
Startled or mischievous, animal-aware
Of my innocence and daring, the pony
Shook his head and side-danced. Old Eagle,
Not yet old, reached to my rescue,
But the pony was off and away over the plain
As if he would never come back.
What could I do but hold onto his mane
And press my moccasined feet to his ribs?
He ran and ran, no gallop, no trot,
But a fierce glad racing, ears back, tail flying,
A fury of pleasure.
Eternal minutes he circled and sped back,
Braking stiff-legged, wall-eyed and panting,
In front of the chief. "Shame!"
In apology the pony lowered his head.
I slid over his brow, undoing the splendor of my feat.

"'Little Cheyenne Riding Like the Wind'
Will be your name."
I listened from the ground.
"This is not your secret dream name.
That you must never tell."
I shall never tell; the name was lost with the dream.

Old Snapshot V

Here is Bakeshop, the town's tramp dog who lived
With us in spring.
He favored us over all others then
For one, only one, thing:
Every evening before twilight we played
Ball in a vacant lot,
Papa, Mama, Sister, I—and this dog
Who never forgot.
He drank root beer, ate handouts, did not beg,
Lived life as he chose:
He elected to be our outfielder,
Athlete from tail to nose;
He ran up under high ones, backed, waited,
Crouched or leaped, and in truth,
He opened his mouth like a fielder's glove,
And never broke a tooth.
At the end of spring training Bakeshop left.
Oh, yes! He chewed gum.
Bakeshop was an individualist,
A tramp dog, not a bum.

Divorce

The old truculent spirit is gone.
This dawn split the one slender flame
Of me into two growing pieces of cool,
Sufficient as each severed piece of worm
That lies on the wet walk after rain.
I even thought of you as one piece
And I the other—once so much a part of each
Until a weariness cut us apart . . .
And now we are free to grow whole again,
After the first few pains of healing.
The old truculent spirit is gone.

XIV.

Reply

How long, how long shall I love you?
As well to ask a stone, a star,
A dying wind in its last breath
How long the days of lovers are.
A shattered wave might answer you,
One that had spent its eager strength
To reach a stretch of fickle sand ...
Breaking its shining self at length.

If I Had Been Less Cautious

If I had been less cautious
Loving you, and broken
Through the fetters of restraint,
Tried less to be honest
With myself and you,
And heedless to tall doubts
That stood close by
When words were near . . .
If I had said just once
"I love you!"
And wondered *after* of its truth . . .
Then I could have kept one thing—
A little glow of words
Strung on a fragile string.

To a New Lover

I have seen dreams in your eyes
And I have asked none.
There are none in my own.
I ask only a moment of love since more is futile.
So many times I have sought to hold
This illusive beauty longer than was meant,
And always I grow tired and turn away . . .
Till now I wonder if I have not been given
A second-hand heart that has never been pleased
And is weary of seeking.
Like a hurdy-gurdy with a sadness
All its own, my heart plays
An old mechanical tune
Because the futility of things
Parades before it always
To laugh a dream away.
So I care not if your eyes are prolific
Of dreams . . .
Give me a moment
To remember . . .
. . . And forget.

A Little Thing

I thought I had forgotten you,
For I could see your face
And hear your voice, and feel
No memories burn . . . and then
Today I saw your hand
Reach out in some familiar way . . .
And the old ache caught in my mind again.

I Wish I Could Remember

I wish that there might come a day
When I could not remember
The gentle flexures of your voice
That made your words so tender.

I wish that I might just forget
For only an hour each day
The tacit understanding
That marked our work and play.

And now my wish comes to me—
The words I thought so tender,
The face of you, the hand of you,
I wish I could remember.

Vagrant Quest

If in some solitary hour
I miss him strangely overmuch,
I may be blind enough to seek
A place made richer by his touch.
I may be lone enough to say:
"That day his cool hand held this book . . .
He turned this page and read this line."
And God knows what it was he took
From me that I should vainly search
In eager half-expectant way
To see his face lost in a crowd . . .
Or find him as the night turns day.

After Grief

Your words are cool winds
Flowing through me.
They are a night wind
Touching me.
I was on a high land
And you sought me.
I was lonely
And you found me.
Now I am quiet
With the cool touch of wind
That is your love
Caressing me.

Lonely

Lonely am I as a lone flag flying
Against the moon.
A song in my throat like a seabird's crying
On a pale dune.
Lonely am I as a sad man's laughter
In a gay room . . .
Wretched with longing that follows after
Fires that consume.

Essence

I am a wind
Blown out of the earth,
The inners of the earth,
Over flowers
That are yet to spring
Up from its edges . . .

I am a wind
Blown through you
Fragrant with swollen seeds,
Strong and free
With the breath
Of things unborn . . .

I am a wind
That bothers the lock
And sends the branch
Catching and troubling
Your roof
In little soft sounds
Like thoughts out of me
That have caught in your mind
And will not lie down . . .

I am a wind
That will trouble
Your door
And never
Come in.

Afterword

The additional selected poems for this new collection were written by Sanora Babb between 1927 and 1989, with the most recent being "My Lost Name" (manuscript dated June 14, 1989). More than half are from the 1920s and '30s, when Babb was most actively publishing poetry. The weighting of this group toward Babb's earlier poems balances that of *Told in the Seed* toward her later years. Thus, *Told in the Seed and Selected Poems* provides a comprehensive selection of Babb's more than sixty years of writing and publishing poetry.

Babb's papers at the Harry Ransom Center in Austin, Texas, include contributor's copies and tear sheets for her published poems and fair copies of finished poems typed by her as well as handwritten drafts. Occasionally Babb made inked or penciled corrections to these and, more rarely, changes to already published poems on the tear sheets or journals themselves. Some unpublished poems appear in multiple drafts both handwritten and typed on the same day, as evidenced by Babb's often meticulous dating when working on drafts. In editing previously unpublished poems for this collection, we have used a light hand. Our goal has been to produce a collection that would appeal to a contemporary reader, not to preserve an archival transcript of Babb's work for scholars. We have made silent corrections whenever Babb misspelled or abbreviated a word in typescript that she elsewhere spelled conventionally or wrote in full. Punctuation of ellipses and within quotation marks has been regularized to contemporary standards. In "One with the Braves" we have gone so far as to modernize Babb's spelling of "pow wow" to "powwow," per preferred contemporary Native usage—a preference we believe Babb herself would have respected. In three cases where unpublished poems did not have titles, we have used the first line as the title, following

Babb's own practice in poems such as "I Thought I Saw the Dawn Go By" and elsewhere.

In every case where Babb made inked corrections to typed drafts or published versions of a poem, we have worked hard to determine her final intention, as indicated by her own editorial markings. Her most extensive editing occurs in "This Is the Time and Place to Write a Poem, I Thought." Babb's typescript includes alternate wording in lines 11, 16, and 20, without indicating her final preference. In this poem and other cases, we have chosen the option that seemed most consistent with the intention of the poem itself or with Babb's typical diction and figuration in her other poems written in the same time period.

Our ability to add new poems to this collection would not have been possible without access to Sanora Babb's archives and the invaluable help from the staff at the Harry Ransom Center at the University of Texas, Austin.

Acknowledgments

"A Little Thing," *Community Arts and Crafts*, 1928.
"Above Malpaso Creek," *Hawaii Review*, 1988.
"Allegro Con Fuoco," *Dalhousie Review*, 1956. Also published as
   "I Ride a Wild Horse," *University of Kansas City Review*, 1955.
"Bird of Night," *University of Kansas City Review*, 1955.
"Captive," *The Harp*, 1932; rpt. in Mitre Press *Spring Anthology*, 1932.
"Coute Que Coute," *The Harp*, 1929.
"Critic," *Kentucky Poetry Review*, 1989-90.
"Essence," *Prairie Schooner*, 1933.
"Fog," *Hollywood Topics of the Town*, 1930.
"For Future Reference," *Stratford Magazine*, 1928; rpt.
   Grub Street Book of Verse, 1928.
"For My Inquisitive Friends," *Hollywood Topics of the Town*, 1931.
"Giant Sequoia," *Outdoor World*, 1970.
"I Had Forgotten," *Contemporary Verse*, 1930.
"I Wish I Could Remember," *The Prism*, 1928; rpt.
   Grub Street Book of Verse, 1928.
"If I Had Been Less Cautious," *Visions*, 1932
"In a Field in Peloponesia," *Arizona Quarterly*, 1981.
"Kansas Prairie," *The Prism*, 1930.
"Lean Away from the Tree," *Southwest Review*, 1975.
"L'Immortelle," *Zero Anthology*, 1956.
"Lonely," *The Kaleidoscope*, 1930.
"Measure," *Clay Magazine*, 1930.
"Night in a Greek Village," *The Southern Review*, 1990.
"Night Visit," *The Southern Review*, 1981.

"Old Snapshots I-III," *Prairie Schooner*, 1955-56.
"Plea," *JAPM (Just Another Poetry Magazine)*, 1932.
"Rain," *The Lantern*, 1930.
"Reply," *Embryo Magazine*, 1930.
"The Last Year," *Hawaii Review*, 1987.
"The Visitor," *Southwest Review*, 1963.
"To a New Lover," *Hollywood Topics of the Town*, 1930.
"To Toby," *The Prism*, 1928.
"Told in the Seed," *The Southern Review*, 1966.
"Unholy Grail," *Stratford Magazine*, 1929-30.
"Vagrant Quest," *Star-Dust, A Journal of Poetry*, 1929.
"Wedding Song," *San Francisco Review*, 1961.
"Why Does the Dog Howl on the Midnight Hill?"
       Dalhousie Review, 1956.

About the Author

Sanora Babb (1907-2005) is the author of seven books, as well as numerous essays, short stories, and poems that were published in literary magazines alongside the work of Ernest Hemingway, Dorothy Parker, Ralph Ellison, Katherine Ann Porter, William Saroyan, and William Carlos Williams. She published her first poem at fourteen in the *Forgan Eagle* and continued to write and publish poetry all her life, winning the Borestone Mountain Poetry Award in 1967 for "Told in the Seed" and the Gold Medal Award in 1932 for "Captive" from the Mitre Press Anthology, London.

Called by Douglas Wixson, author of *Worker Writer in America*, "a writer of great skill and humanity . . . a lyric poet of great sensitivity," Babb possessed a strong empathy with people and their daily lives, an affinity with all in the natural world, and the ability to elevate the ordinary into the extraordinary. This is reflected in her poems that quicken with lyricism, clarity, and a sense of immediacy.

About the Editors

Joanne Dearcopp is a writer's coach and Sanora Babb's literary executor, agent, and long-time personal friend. She has worked at Simon & Schuster, McCall Books, and Grolier Publishing. Now, as the publisher of Muse Ink Press, she has brought Babb's previously published books back into print, and continues her endeavors to promote Babb's rediscovery. Joanne is a co-editor of *Unknown No More: Recovering Sanora Babb*, published by the University of Oklahoma Press.

Carol S. Loranger has taught later-19th and 20th century American literature and culture at Wright State University. She has published on the poetry of Sanora Babb, Paul Lawrence Dunbar, Robert Frost, and E.A. Robinson, and on the fiction of writers as diverse as Louisa May Alcott, Theodore Dreiser, Thomas Pynchon, and William S. Burroughs. A sometime poet, she has published poetry as Carol Schaechterle in *Pebble*, *Mad River Review*, *Midwest Review*, and *Louisville Review*.

CPSIA information can be obtained
at www.ICGtesting.com
Printed in the USA
LVHW091116200921
698259LV00011B/195